TULIP

TULIP

*The Five Points
of Calvinism in the Light
of Scripture*

2^d EDITION

Duane Edward Spencer

Baker Books

A Division of Baker Book House Co
Grand Rapids, Michigan 49516

Copyright © 1979 by Baker Books
a division of Baker Book House Company
P.O. Box 6287, Grand Rapids, MI 49516-6287

Twenty-first printing, November 2001

Printed in the United States of America

ISBN 0-8010-6393-0

Library of Congress Cataloging-in-Publication Data is on file at the Library
of Congress, Washington, D.C.

Scripture is from the King James Version of the Bible.

For current information about all releases from Baker Book House, visit our
web site:
                    http://www.bakerbooks.com

Contents

Foreword
Luder G. Whitlock, Jr.

Why should you be interested in reading about the Five Points of Calvinism, a doctrinal formula dating to a seventeenth-century controversy? Because the issue is as relevant today as it was then: how personal freedom of choice relates to divine sovereignty as it finds expression in God's plan for and our experience of salvation.

Although the five points, often referred to as TULIP, are usually associated with the great Reformation theologian John Calvin, they did not originate with him. Rather the followers of Jacob Arminius, a Dutch theologian, expressed their disagreement with the prevailing confessional position in Holland by way of a formal protest, or Remonstrance, which they presented to their Parliament in 1610. At a synod meeting held in Dort in 1618 the five major objections of the Remonstrants were thoroughly discussed and firmly rejected point by point. Their response is usually referred to as "The Five Points of Calvinism." In this volume these two opposing positions are succinctly explained, analyzed, and evaluated.

It is also worth noting, without elaboration, that the conflict between St. Augustine and Pelagius during the fifth century when Pelagius insisted on basic human goodness and individual capability to obey and believe has marked similarities to that which spawned the five points.

Because the five points were a response to the Remonstrants, they are limited in scope, reminding us that even a good defense may not necessarily offer the best offense. Reformed theology, comprehensive and compelling in its profundity, must not be confined to this framework. John Calvin chose a different approach to explain the biblical message as may be observed in his *Institutes of the Christian Religion* and other writings.

On the other hand, the five points do justice to distinctive features of Reformed theology such as the greatness of God, a welcome emphasis since the sovereignty of God has been out of favor in the United States. Beginning early in the nineteenth century, a proclivity for personal freedom and rampant individualism contributed to a democratizing of American Christianity, greatly diminishing God's power in the perception of the average Christian. This populistic influence fueled anti-Reformed sentiments.

Recently there has been a widespread resurgence of interest in Reformed theology, stimulated in part by the rapid deterioration of American culture and a gradual realization within evangelical circles that the most coherent and compelling response to this alarming secularization is offered by the Reformed worldview.

This book demonstrates how the Scriptures speak clearly and forcefully to each of the five points in question, enabling you to ascertain the biblical teaching regarding each one. As you do so one fact is clear: The Lord reigns. Because the Lord God omnipotent reigns we should let God be God, acknowledging and rejoicing in His sovereign love and grace. It surely follows that your salvation is of grace—all of grace—not of works so that you will have no basis to boast (Eph. 8:10).

Finally, you will be able to delight in the fact that if God is for you then it does not matter who is against you because no one can stay His hand (Rom. 8:31). When the power brokers of this world oppose Him, He laughs (Ps. 2). In the all-sufficient grace of a sovereign God you find sure help, undying hope, and enduring security.

If that appeals to you—read on.

Preface

One of the most exciting signs of our time is the increasing interest in the study of the Word of God and in the biblical theology of the Reformation. Instead of the mundane literature of their forebears, many young people are reading such books as *The Bondage of the Will* by Martin Luther and *The Institutes* of John Calvin. As they read and compare the theology of the Protestant Reformers with their Bibles, they begin to realize that much of the theology of contemporary *evangelism* has neglected grace and emphasized the works of the flesh. If they go so far as to study the history of theology they also learn that the doctrine of most "evangelical" churches today is the humanist theology of Erasmus of Rome. It is then that they begin to see just why fundamentalists and liberals, Protestants and Catholics, high church and pentecostals can work side by side in the major revivals and crusades of the twentieth century. That which they hold in common is the exalted doctrine of man espoused by Erasmus, sharply defined by Arminius, made popular by the Wesleys, and given a final polish by many religious psychologists of our time.

Strange as it may seem there are many today who insist that they believe in salvation by grace, yet they insist that man has the power to "make a decision for Christ." They argue that "God loves everyone, equally and alike," yet they are sure that He is going to send some people to hell. They affirm that the Bible teaches that the Creator of all things is surely *omnipotent,* but they are also quite confident that finite man is fully capable of obstructing the will of God. In nearly every case the problem lies in the fact that these dear people do not know Bible doctrine. They have heard nothing from their pulpits but "plan of salvation" sermons *minus* the doctrines that make up the *plan!* If they were asked to explain the meaning of such doctrines as redemption, propitiation, reconciliation, remission, and atonement, they would either mutter trivia or be absolutely speechless. Why? Because they have never been taught, nor have they had the spiritual vigor necessary to discover for themselves, what Scripture teaches about the work of Christ. There is one thing they hold in common: the confidence that man can use his own *positive volition* to accept Christ and get himself "saved."

Many Baptists who think they are anti-Calvinists are not aware of the fact that one of their greatest preachers, Charles Haddon Spurgeon, was a solid five-point Calvinist. The golden-tongued preacher said:

> The old truth that Calvin preached, that Augustine preached, that Paul preached, is the truth that I must preach today, or else be false to my conscience and my God. I cannot *shape* the truth. I know of no such thing as paring off the rough edges of a doctrine. John Knox's gospel is my gospel. That which thundered through Scotland must thunder through England again.

Throughout history many of the great evangelists, missionaries, and stalwart theologians held to the precious doctrines of grace known as Calvinism. For example,

William Carey stood solidly for predestination but did not hesitate to call on men to repent of their sins and trust in Christ. The sovereignty of God and the responsibility of man to believe the Word of God are not at all incompatible doctrines. Once the basic teachings of Calvinism are correctly understood, the heart becomes warm, and the urgency of sharing the gospel with others becomes almost overwhelming. Burns of China, M'Cheyne, Whitfield, Brainerd, Bonar, Luther, Knox, Latimer, Tyndale, Rutherford, Bunyan, Goodwin, Owen, Watson, Watts, Newton, Hodge, Warfield, and Pink are only a few of the pulpit giants whose preaching shone with the doctrines of sovereign grace. All of them would voice a fervent amen to these words of Spurgeon:

> I love to proclaim those strong old doctrines nicknamed Calvinism, but which are surely and verily the revealed truth of God as it is in Christ Jesus.

The Five Points of Arminianism

A Dutch theologian named Jacob Hermann, who lived from 1560 to 1609, was best known by the Latin form of his last name, *Arminius*. Although reared in the Reformed tradition, Arminius leaned toward the humanist doctrines of Erasmus, for he had serious doubts about *sovereign grace* as it was preached by the Reformers. His disciples, called *Arminians* and *Remonstrants,* expanded the teaching of their master. Several years after his death they formulated his doctrines into five main points known as the *Five Points of Arminianism.*

Since the churches of the Netherlands, in common with the other major Protestant churches of Europe, had subscribed to the Reformed Doctrines of the Belgic and Heidelberg Confessions, the Arminians determined to present the Dutch Parliament with a *Remonstrance.* This carefully written protest of the Reformed faith was submitted to the State of Holland and, in 1618, a National Synod of the Church was convened in Dort to examine the teachings of Arminius in the light of Scripture. After 154 earnest sessions, which lasted seven months, the *Five Points of Arminianism* were found con-

13

trary to Scripture and declared heretical. At the same time the theologians of the church reaffirmed the position held by the Protestant Reformers as consistent with Scripture and formulated what is known as *The Five Points of Calvinism* (in honor of the great French theologian, John Calvin).

Over the years the studied reply of the Synod of Dort to the heresies of Arminius has been set forth in the form of an acrostic forming the word TULIP (hence the name of this little book). The five points are:

T—Total depravity
U—Unconditional election
L—Limited atonement
I—Irresistible grace
P—Perseverance of the saints

Since we shall be examining in some detail what the Reformation theologians of Dort meant by these five points, let us first take a look at a summary of the *Five Points of Arminianism.*

I

FREE WILL. The first point of Arminianism was that man possesses free will. The Reformers acknowledged that man had a will, but they agreed with Luther's thesis in his book *The Bondage of the Will* that it was *not* free from bondage to Satan. Arminius believed that the fall of man was not total, holding that there was enough good left in man for him to will to accept Christ unto salvation.

II

CONDITIONAL ELECTION. Arminius further taught that election was based upon the foreknowledge of God as to who would believe. In other words man's *act of faith* is the "condition" for his being elected to eternal life, since God foresaw him exercising his "free will" in positive volition toward Christ.

III

UNIVERSAL ATONEMENT. Inasmuch as it was their further conviction that God loves everybody, that Christ died for everyone, and that the Father is not willing that any should perish, Arminius and his followers held that redemption (used casually as a synonym for atonement) was general. In other words the death of Christ provided grounds for God to save all men. However, each must exercise his *free will* to accept Christ.

IV

OBSTRUCTABLE GRACE. The Arminian further believed that since God wanted all men to be saved, He sent the Holy Spirit to woo all men to Christ. However, since man has absolute "free will" he is able to resist God's will for his life (the Arminian order being that man exercises his own will first, *then* he is born again). Although the Arminian says he believes that God is omnipotent, he insists that God's will to save all men can be frustrated by the finite will of man on an individual basis.

15

V

FALLING FROM GRACE. The fifth point of Arminianism is the logical outcome of the preceding portions of the system. If man cannot be saved by God unless it is man's will to be saved, then man cannot *continue* in salvation unless he continues to will to be saved.

The Contrast

As you contrast the five points of Arminianism with the acrostic forming TULIP, it is apparent that the *Five Points of Calvinism* are diametrically opposed to the *Five Points of Arminianism*. That we may see clearly "the lines of battle" as drawn by the keen minds of both camps, let us start by making a brief contrast between the two positions on a point-by-point basis.

POINT ONE. The **Arminian** says that man's will is "free" to choose either the Word of God or the word of Satan. Salvation, therefore, is dependent upon *man's work* of faith.

The **Calvinist** responds that unregenerate man is in absolute bondage to Satan and wholly incapable of exercising his own will freely to trust in Christ. Salvation, therefore, is dependent upon the work of God who must will to give man life *before* he can believe in Christ.

POINT TWO. **Arminius** held that election was conditional, while the Reformers declared it to be *unconditional*. The Arminians believed that God elected those whom He "foreknew" would believe unto salvation, so that foreknowledge was based upon a *condition* established by man.

The **Calvinists** held that "foreknowledge" was based upon the purpose or plan of God, so that election had no basis in some fancied condition on the part of man, but was the result of the free will of the Creator apart from any foreseen "work of faith" in spiritually dead man.

Again it will be noted that the second position of each party is the natural outcome of its doctrine of man. If man does have free will and is not in bondage to Satan and sin, then he is able to provide the condition whereby God may elect to save him. However, if man does not have free will, but is actually in bondage to Satan and sin, then his only hope is that God has chosen of His *free will* to elect him to salvation.

POINT THREE. The **Arminian** insists that *atonement* (and by that he means redemption) is *universal*. The **Calvinist** insists that redemption is particular, which is to say *limited atonement* was made by Christ at the cross.

1. *ARMINIANISM*—Christ died to save *no one in particular,* but only those who exercise their free will and accept His offer of eternal life. Hence His death was a partial failure since those with negative volition will go to hell.
2. *CALVINISM*—Christ died to save *particular persons* who were given Him by the Father in eternity past. His death was, therefore, a 100 percent success, in that all for whom He died will be saved, and all for whom He did not die will receive "justice" from God when they are cast into hell.

POINT FOUR. The **Arminian** continues by stating that although the Holy Spirit seeks to woo all men to Christ (since God loves all mankind and wills to save all men), still, since the will of God is bound by the will of man, the Spirit can be resisted by man if man so chooses. Since man alone can determine whether he will be saved or not, it stands to reason that God at least permits man to obstruct His holy will. He is willing to be impotent in the face of man's will so that the creature may "be as God," just as Satan promised Eve in the garden.

The **Calvinist** replies that the grace of God cannot be obstructed, but that the Lord possesses "irresistible grace." By this he does not mean that Jehovah crushes man's obstinate will like a giant steamroller! *Irresistible grace* is not grounded in the omnipotence of God, although it could be if the Lord so willed, but, rather, in the gift of life known as *regeneration*. Since all *dead* human spirits are drawn irresistibly to Satan, the god of the dead, and all *living* human spirits are drawn irresistibly to Jehovah, the God of the living, our Lord simply gives His chosen ones the Spirit of life! The moment He does so their spiritual polarity is changed. Where they were once "dead in trespasses and sins" and oriented to the devil, now they are made "alive in Christ Jesus" and oriented to God.

It is at this point that another great difference between Arminian theology and Calvinist theology becomes apparent. The **Arminian** says that the order of events is: *First,* man's work of faith, next, God's gift of life. The **Calvinist** declares that the order of events is: *First,* God's gift of life, then saving faith.

POINT FIVE. Finally, the **Arminian** concludes (quite logically) that since man is saved by his own act of free will in accepting Christ, he can be lost (after he has been saved), by changing his mind about Christ. Some Arminians would add that he can subsequently lose his salvation by committing some sin, since Arminian theology is a "works theology"—at least to the extent that man must exercise his own will in order to be saved. This possibility of being lost, after once having been saved, is called "falling from grace" by the followers of Arminius. Again, if after being saved, then becoming lost, a person should freely will to turn to Christ again, repenting of his sins, he could then "get saved again." It all depends upon man's continuing positive volition until he dies.

The **Calvinist** replies quite simply, since salvation is entirely the work of the Lord, and man has absolutely nothing to do with "getting saved" in the first place, it is obvious that "keeping saved" is also the work of God, apart from any good or bad on the part of His elect. The saints will "persevere" for the simple reason that God promises this, assuring us that He will finish the work He has begun in us! Hence, point five of TULIP speaks of the perseverance of the saints.

The Will of God

Let us begin our comparison of the *Five Points of Armini-anism* and the *Five Points of Calvinism* with Scripture by establishing the biblical view of the will and decree of God. When we speak of the "will" of Jehovah we must remember that it is but the expression of His omnipotent, omniscient Being. If He is *omnipotent*, as Scripture testifies, He will achieve all that He purposes, and, if He is *omniscient*, He will make no mistakes in His original plan, nor will he ever find it necessary to alter His original purpose.

> "Known unto God are all his works from the beginning of the world" (Acts 15:18).

As Benjamin Warfield has carefully stated: "In the infinite wisdom of the Lord of all the earth, each event falls with exact precision into its proper place in the unfolding of His divine plan. Nothing, however small, however strange, occurs without His ordering, or without its particular fitness for its place in the working out of His purpose; and the end of all shall be the manifestation of His glory, and the accumulation of His praise. This is the Old Testament (as well as the New Testament)

21

philosophy of the universe—a world-view which attains concrete unity in an absolute decree, or *Purpose,* or plan, of which all that comes to pass is but its development in time."

Therefore, as we shall see, whatever comes to pass in the history of mankind does so by virtue of the fact that it suited the eternal plan or purpose of God. Should anything take place contrary to the will of God, because in the opinion of the finite creature it is not "good," then Satan and man (on occasion at least) must be equal or superior to the Creator whose Word claims that He is omnipotent and wholly irresistible! On the other hand, if the determinitive will of Jehovah reflects His immutable nature of Being, it can neither be obstructed nor canceled. Therefore, whatever comes to pass in any part of creation, at any time in history, does so because the omniscient God knew it as a possibility, willed it as a reality by His omnipotence, and established it in His divine plan or purpose.

It will be further seen that there is no conflict between those mighty works which manifest His holiness, righteousness, and wrath, and those glorious works which display His grace, love, and forgiveness. In the light of the whole of Scripture, Jehovah will be seen consistent as He damns some and forgives others, as He displays His sovereign righteousness and justice toward unrepentant sinners, while declaring His sovereign grace, freely forgiving all whom He chose "in Christ Jesus" before the foundation of the world. As the only genuinely *Free Agent* in all of eternity, who, alone is not influenced by any creature or outside force, the Lord of the Glory can bluntly say:

> "I will have mercy on whom I will have mercy, and I will have compassion on whom I will have compassion" (Rom. 9:15).

As the only Being in time and eternity with absolute free-dom to will as He sees fit, God has laid out a plan which includes both election and reprobation. Paul says:

> "And not only this; but when Rebecca also had conceived by one, even by our father Isaac; (For the children being not yet born, neither having done any good or evil, that the *purpose* of God *according to election* might stand, not of works, but of him that *calleth;*) It was said unto her, The elder shall serve the younger. As it is written, Jacob have I loved, but Esau have I hated" (Rom. 9:10–13).

In other words, without taking into account either "good" or "bad" in the two men, God made Jacob the object of His love and Esau the object of His wrath. Why? So that His *purpose* or divine plan, in keeping with "election" (or choosing of persons and events that ful-fill His will) might stand. The God of Scripture makes no apologies for the fact that He determined to let most men spend eternity under His wrath, giving them exactly what they deserve, while He has also determined to ordain unto salvation some who are equally deserving of wrath, because it pleases Him to do so that He might display His nature of grace, mercy, and love in the pres-ence of the elect angels. This is why Paul can say:

> "For God hath not appointed us to wrath, but [He hath appointed us] to obtain salvation by our Lord Jesus Christ" (1 Thess. 5:9).

Christ is indeed a scandal to the unregenerate and would be such to all men if God had not chosen to regenerate some, bringing them to repentance and giving them faith in His Word. Peter says that the Savior is

23

"a stone of stumbling, and a rock of offence, even to them which stumble at the word, being disobedient; whereunto also *they were appointed*" (1 Peter 2:8).

Here he uses the same Greek word for *appointed* as Paul uses when he says that we, to the contrary, were "not appointed" to wrath and unbelief.

When the apostle Paul wishes to show how God ordained some to salvation, wholly apart from any qualities of good on their part, whereas He appointed others to condemnation, he says:

"The scripture saith unto Pharaoh, Even for this same *purpose* have I raised thee up, that I might shew my power in thee, and that my name might be declared throughout all the earth" (Rom. 9:17).

In other words, when God needed someone for His plan who would resist His word and pursue Israel to slay the people of God, He chose Pharaoh. Out of the millions of sperm that might have joined with the waiting egg in Pharaoh's mother, God determined which one would be joined to become the king of Egypt. That particular individual was perfectly fitted for the task of performing those deeds that would fitly fulfill the purpose of God in that striking moment of history. Jehovah, to fulfill His plan, did not force Pharaoh to act contrary to his nature. He simply raised up a person who had all of the necessary ingredients whereby he would will to respond positively to "the Prince of the power of the air" and, at the same instant, fulfill the divine purpose established in eternity past! This is but the enunciation of the principle,

"Surely the wrath of man shall praise [Jehovah]" (Psalm 76:10).

Before He ever laid out the heavens and the earth, the Creator determined that every creature and every act of history should be to His glory and honor and to none other. He also determined that

> "at the name of Jesus every knee should bow, of things in heaven, and things in earth, and things under the earth, and that every tongue should confess that Jesus Christ is Lord, to the glory of God the Father" (Phil. 2:10–11).

Furthermore, to those who find fault with the eternal decree, Paul writes:

> "Nay but, O man, who art thou that repliest against God? Shall the thing formed say to him that formed it, Why hast thou made me thus? Hath not the potter power over the clay, of the same lump to make one vessel unto honour, and another unto dishonour? What if God, willing to show his wrath, and to make his power known, endured with much long-suffering the vessels of wrath *fitted* ["appointed"] *to destruction;* and that he might make known the riches of *his glory* on the vessels of mercy, which he had afore *prepared unto glory,* even *us* whom *he hath called . . .*" (Rom. 9:20–24).

In short, the Divine Potter predestined that some of His creatures should be fitted or "appointed" to be vessels of dishonor, whose end would be eternal wrath. Others (made of the same clay) should be predestined to be vessels suited to bring glory to His name and ordained to spend eternity in the bliss of heaven. My! If Paul were preaching such a message in the average "evangelical" pulpit today there would be a meeting of the officers and a casting out of the preacher before they took time for the lunch they normally rush out to eat! No wonder the Scripture says:

> "My thoughts are not your thoughts, neither are your ways my ways, saith the LORD. For as the heavens are higher than the earth, so are my ways higher than your ways, and my thoughts than your thoughts" (Isa. 55:8–9).

Certainly the way of God is not the "way that seemeth right unto a man"! However, remember, the way that seems so right to the reason of man is actually the way of Satan and ends in eternal death (cf. Prov. 14:12).

Men may connive and scheme, following the counter plan of their god, Satan, but they cannot bring to pass so much as one act contrary to the will and plan of God who foreordained all of history from the largest event to the most insignificant. As a result the saints of God can "in all things give thanks" for they know that the Creator has laid out a plan that guarantees that "all things" of history shall work together for the good of His elect. They can face their enemies who have sought to ruin their lives, as well as events which have been distressing and painful, and say with Joseph of old:

> "Ye thought evil against me, but God meant it unto good" (Gen. 50:20).

Like Nebuchadnezzar, after his sanity was regained, we must understand that

> "All the inhabitants of the earth are reputed as nothing: [Jehovah] doeth according to his will in the army of heaven, and among the inhabitants of the earth: and *none can stay his hand,* or say to him, What doest thou?" (Dan. 4:35).

Loraine Boettner has summed it up, "Everything was infallibly determined and immutably fixed by God from the beginning, and all that happens in time is but the accomplishment of what was ordained in eternity."

Jehovah says:

> "I am God and there is none like me, declaring the end from the beginning, and from ancient times the things that are not yet done. My counsel shall stand, and I will do all my pleasure: . . . I have spoken it, I will bring it to pass. I have *purposed* it, I will also do it" (Isa. 46:9–11).

How ego-withering is such testimony! How the carnal mind of man loathes the doctrines of sovereign grace and retribution! How his heart rebels against the decrees of the Almighty who rules without His immutable will ever being violated! How he hates to be told:

> "A man's heart deviseth his way: but the Lord directeth his steps" (Prov. 16:9).

The carnal mind seeks to create its own god which loves everyone, puts up with all manner of evil and foolishness, and gives in to the will of evil men who cry "Inequality!" Sinful man cannot tolerate a God who will say:

> "Go, and tell this people, Hear ye indeed, but understand not; and see ye, indeed, but perceive not. Make the heart of this people fat, and make their ears heavy, and shut their eyes; lest they see with their eyes, and hear with their ears, and understand with their heart, and convert, and be healed" (Isa. 6:9–10).

Yet this is precisely the God we have in Scripture, whether we view Him through the Old Testament prophets, or in the person of His dear Son in the New Testament. As Luther bluntly put it: "This mightily offends our rational nature, that God should, of His own mere unbiased will, leave some men to themselves, harden them, and then condemn them; but He has given abundant demonstration, and does continually, that this is really the case, namely, that the sole cause why some are saved and others perish proceeds from His willing the salvation of the former and the perdition of the latter."

"Therefore hath he mercy on whom he will have mercy, and whom he will he hardeneth" (Rom. 9:18).

God's Word is His power unto salvation to all who believe. He determines who shall believe and who shall not believe. God declares:

"So shall my word be that goeth forth out of my mouth: it shall not return unto me void, but it shall accomplish *that which I please,* and it shall prosper *whereto I sent it*" (Isa. 55:11).

Note! The will of God is accomplished by the Word of God whenever it is sent forth. Two men, perhaps identical twins, are seated in church as they attend the preaching of the Word of God. One yields to Christ and the other rejects the Savior. Why? (Take care not to answer on the basis of human reasoning but on the basis of Scripture!) According to the Bible the Word of God accomplishes the will of God. It stands, therefore, that the one man "believes" because such was the will of God, and the other rejects because that, too, was the will of God.

Were it not for the divine choosings and the election of some to salvation, none would ever believe. Only those who are "ordained unto salvation" believe, for the Word of God never returns empty handed, frustrated, and defeated. It always, and without exception, accomplishes the pleasure of the sovereign God, because He has decreed that His divine plan shall prosper in each single detail (cf. Acts 13:48).

I

Total Depravity

The first of the *Five Points of Calvinism* is easily remembered under the "T" of the acrostic forming the word TULIP. "T" stands for *total depravity*.

To properly understand the doctrine of salvation we must discover what is the doctrine of man according to Scripture. Does the Bible agree with the Arminian position that man is not totally fallen, or does it declare that he is totally depraved (i.e., completely unable to cope with his sinful state in order to gain, or contribute to, his own salvation)? J. C. Ryle has aptly stated:

> "There are very few errors and false doctrines of which the beginning may not be traced up to unsound views about the corruption of human nature. Wrong views of the disease will always bring with them wrong views of the remedy. Wrong views of the corruption of human nature will always carry with them wrong views of the grand antidote and cure of that corruption."

Fully aware that to begin with a false hypothesis must mean to end with a terrible heresy, the august theologians of the Synod of Dort formulated the first point of the *Five Points of Calvinism* in reply to the Remonstrants' *Five Points of Arminianism*. Man, they said, was "totally depraved."

Now, the point is, what did the Reformation theologians mean by this term *total depravity?* Perhaps we can best answer by stating what the term does *not* mean. It does not mean "absolute depravity." This latter term means that one expresses the evil of his sin nature as much as possible at all times. "Total depravity," furthermore, does not mean that man is incapable of human good. We all know that the most wicked of mankind have some human good about them, just as the finest among mankind have some human bad about them. We have all read stories of gangsters, liquor barons, prostitutes and pimps, along with dope peddlers and the like, who have done deeds of human good. No, the Reformation doctrine of the *total depravity of man* does not seek to say that there is no *human* "good" in man. When man measures himself by man he is always able to find some good in himself or in others.

Total depravity, according to the giants of the Protestant Reformation (such as Luther, Calvin, and Knox), meant that man was as *bad off* as man could be. It meant that man was beyond all self-help because, as Paul puts it, he is born into this world "dead in trespasses and sins" and, therefore, fully loyal to Satan, the god of the dead. Hence the apostle's argument:

> "Ye walked according to the course of this world, according to the prince of the power of the air, the spirit that now worketh in the *children of disobedience* . . . fulfilling the desires of the flesh and of the mind; and were by nature the *children of wrath*" (Eph. 2:2–3).

Man's depravity, or *total inability* to deliver himself from bondage to sin, is grounded in the fact that his human *spirit* is dead from birth.

Total depravity means that man in his natural state is incapable of doing anything or desiring anything pleasing to God. Until he is "born again" of the Holy Spirit and given a living human spirit, man is the slave of Satan ("the Prince of the power of the air") who drives man to fulfill the desires of the flesh that are in enmity with God. In the sight of God the "best hearted man" holds only evil thoughts because they are oriented to doing *human* good for the glory of himself or Satan but never for the glory of the Creator. In fact he is well described in the words of Scripture:

> "every imagination of the thoughts of his heart was only evil *continually*" (Gen. 6:5).

Total depravity declares that man may think that his heart holds much "good," but the Bible says:

> "The heart is deceitful above all things, and desperately wicked: who can know it?" (Jer. 17:9).

From the divine viewpoint, men are under condemnation because they love sin, for sin is disobedience to the will of God and falling short of giving God all of the glory. When man insists that he still has a spark of divine good resident in his heart, and that he is seeking after God, the Word of God answers:

> "There is none righteous, no, not one: There is none that understandeth, there is *none that seeketh* after God" (Rom. 3:10–11).

As man is viewed from God's exalted position of absolute righteousness and holiness, His Word declares:

> "This is the condemnation, that light is come into the world, and *men loved darkness* rather than light, because their deeds were evil" (John 3:19).

Man is *totally depraved* in the sense that everything about his nature is in rebellion against God. Man is loyal to the god of darkness and loves darkness rather than The Light. His will is, therefore, not at all "free." It is bound by the flesh to the prince of darkness grim. *Total depravity* means that man, of his own "free will," will never make a decision for Christ. Even our blessed Lord bluntly says:

> "Ye *will not* come to me, that ye might have life" (John 5:40).

Why does our Lord say this? Because the *will* of unregenerate man is *bound* by the bands of sin and death to the god of the spiritually dead. They are, as Paul said to Timothy, in the "snare of the devil" and "taken captive by [Satan] at his will" (cf. 2 Tim. 2:26).

Total depravity means that the natural man is completely incapable of discerning truth. In fact, unregenerate man thinks of the things of God as being ridiculous!

> "The natural [i.e., soulish] man *receiveth not* the things of the Spirit of God: for they are foolishness unto him: *neither can he know them,* because they are spiritually discerned" (1 Cor. 2:14).

Total depravity agrees with Holy Scripture. Man cannot see or know the things that relate to the kingdom of God,

34

without being regenerated first by the Holy Spirit. A dead spirit perceives only the things of man and Satan. Hence the words of our Lord to Nicodemus:

> "Except a man be born again, *he cannot see* the kingdom of God" (John 3:3).

Unborn children do not see the light. Dead men do not see the light. Natural (soulish) unregenerate men cannot comprehend the things of God. They are the unborn dead (spiritually) who know only darkness. They are totally depraved, wholly incapable of thinking, perceiving, or doing anything pleasing to God, until God sees fit to give them life and understanding. Faith follows the giving of life. The giving of life is by the will of God. Notice the order:

> "God, who is rich in mercy, for his great love wherewith he loved *us,* even when *we were dead* in sins, hath quickened us together with Christ, (by grace are ye saved;)" (Eph. 2:4–5).

Man is not *saved* by some mythical act of his own *free will.* He is saved by the grace ("unmerited favor") of God who first gives him *life* and *then* instills faith in his heart as a free gift. Paul continues:

> "For by grace are ye saved through faith; and that *not of yourselves:* it is the *gift of God:* Not of works, lest any man should boast" (Eph. 2:8–9).

Observe! Salvation is the gift of God. It is not the work of man. God has decreed that the *works* of the flesh shall have no part in the "so great salvation" which He Himself provides. It is His work through the gift of life. He regenerated us when we were yet dead in sins. Faith, too, is His gift. We are saved by means of faith "which is not of ourselves."

Total depravity insists that man does not have a "free will" in the sense that he is *free* to trust Jesus Christ as his Lord and Savior. This first point, in reply to the *Five Points of Arminianism,* argues that the Scriptures teach that man is the slave of sin, that he is spiritually dead, that he loves darkness rather than light, and that he can "hear" only the voice of Satan—*unless* God gives him ears to hear and eyes to see, because it pleases Him so to do (cf. Prov. 20:12). Hence the words of Jesus:

> "Why do ye not understand my speech? Even because ye *cannot* hear my word! Ye are of your father the devil" (John 8:43–44).

Total depravity means that unregenerate man is hopelessly enmeshed in sin, bound by Satan with the cords of spiritual death, and wholly disinterested in the things of the Creator. When the time comes that those bonds are broken and death replaced by eternal life, it is the work of God who, alone, gives the faith that desires and does those things pleasing to Him. This is why Paul tells the elect,

> "It is God which worketh in you both to *will* and to *do* of his good pleasure" (Phil. 2:13).

Just as Lazarus would never have heard the voice of Jesus, nor would he have ever "come to Jesus" without first being given life by our Lord, so all men "dead in trespasses and sins" must first be given life by God before they can "come to Christ." Since dead men cannot *will* to receive life but can be raised from the dead only by the power of God, so the natural man cannot of his own (mythical) "free will" *will* to have eternal life (cf. John 10:26–28).

Total depravity declares that lost man's only hope is in an election based on the purpose or plan of God. Only those who are "of God" *hear* the voice of God calling them to "come forth" (by name)! Jesus said to those who did not believe on Him:

> "He that is of God hears God's words: ye therefore hear them not, because ye are not of God" (John 8:47).

II

Unconditional Election

The second of the *Five Points of Calvinism* is easily remembered under the letter "U" of the acrostic forming the word TULIP. That "U" stands for *unconditional election.* This doctrine is set forth in the *Baptist Confession of Faith of 1689* in terms almost identical to those of the Westminster Confession and the Thirty-nine Articles of the Church of England, as well as the Heidelberg and Belgic Confessions and the Canons of Dort.

> "Those of mankind who are *predestinated* unto Life, God, before the foundation of the world was laid, according to His eternal and *immutable Purpose,* and the secret *counsel* and good pleasure of *His will,* hath *chosen* in Christ to everlasting glory, out of His mere free grace and love, without any other thing in the creature as a *condition* or cause moving Him thereunto."

As we think of this point we will remember that the Arminian view is that *foreknowledge* is based upon the positive act of man's will as the *condition* or cause that moved God to elect him to salvation. All of the great confessions, in agreement with the Protestant Reformers, declare that election is "unconditional." In other words, the *foreknowledge* of God is based upon His decree, plan, or purpose that expresses His will, and not upon some foreseen act of *positive volition* on the part of man. We must turn our attention, therefore, to Scripture to discover whether *foreknowledge* is based upon the will and purpose of man or upon the will and purpose of God. Paul states:

> "We *know* that all things work together for good to them that love God, to them who are *the called* according to his *purpose*. For whom he *did foreknow*, he also did predestinate . . ." (Rom. 8:28–29).

Here we see that *election* is based upon the divine plan ("according to His purpose") so that *foreknowledge*, too, must be founded upon the *purpose* of God and not upon the *works* of the elect. This is why Paul also states:

> "For the children being not yet born, neither having done any good or evil, that the *purpose* of God according to *election* might stand, *not of works*, but of him that *calleth*; . . . it is written, Jacob have I loved, but Esau have I hated" (Rom. 9:11).

Here the apostle declares that the ground of election is in God Himself, which is to say in His will and purpose, and not in an act of faith or some *"condition"* (as Arminius would say) in the children for good or evil. Election is *unconditional.* Man can do nothing to merit it.

[handwritten margin note: ELECTION IS GOD'S PREFERENCE FOR THE BELIEVER: FOR HIS BELIEF W/O REF TO HIS WORKS]

The Scriptures stress that God does not elect persons to be saved *because* of some goodness or greatness foreseen in them. On the contrary, He delights in using the weak, base, and useless in a way that guarantees that He alone will gain the glory!

> "See your *calling*, brethren, how that not many wise men after the flesh, not many mighty, not many noble, *are called:* But *God hath chosen the foolish things* of the world to confound the wise; and *God hath chosen the weak things* of the world to confound the things which are mighty; and *base* things of the world, and things which are *despised*, hath God chosen, yea, and things which are not, to bring to nought things that are: *That no flesh should glory in his presence*" (1 Cor. 1:26–29).

In his letter to Timothy he reaffirms *unconditional election* when he writes:

> "[God] hath saved us, and *called* us with an holy calling, not according to our works, but according to *his own purpose* and grace, which was given us in Christ Jesus before the world began . . ." (2 Tim. 1:9).

Again, our calling or "election" is not conditioned by something that man does for God (such as exercising positive volition) but "according to his own purpose." Election is "unconditional" as far as man's works are concerned.

However, the bluntest affirmation that man does not do the choosing of God, since his depraved nature is capable of being "positive" only toward Satan, is that of Jesus who testified:

> "Ye have not chosen me, but I have chosen you" (John 15:16).

41

In fact, according to Paul, that *choice* was made by God before He ever made so much as one single thing!

> "According as *he hath chosen us* in [Christ] before the foundation of the world" (Eph. 1:4).

It is tantamount to blasphemy for anyone to argue that man is capable, of his own free will, to make a decision for Christ, when the Son of God says in words that cannot be misunderstood:

> "No man can come to me, except the Father . . . draw him" (John 6:44).

Only those whom the Father saw fit to choose of His free will, apart from any condition on their part, are given faith to believe unto salvation. Note the clear testimony of Luke:

> "And when the Gentiles heard this, they were glad, and glorified the word of the Lord: *and as many as were ordained to eternal life believed*" (Acts 13:48).

The Lord Jesus insists that life and faith are the work of God, *not* the work of man. He says:

> "The Son quickeneth whom he will"

and

> "This is the *work of God,* that ye *believe* on him whom he hath sent" (John 5:21; 6:29).

In all fairness, the evangelist who says to the crowd, "Whosoever comes to Jesus will in no wise be cast out," should add the preceding words of Christ:

42

"All that the Father giveth me shall come to me . . ." (John 6:37).

Who is it that will not be cast out? All who come to Him! Who, then, will come to the Savior? He says, "All that the Father giveth me." The *choice* as to who will come to Christ is God's, not man's.

Actually there is a splendid view of *unconditional election* given by our Lord when He said to the leaders of Israel:

> "I tell you . . . many widows were in Israel in the days of Elias . . . But unto none of them was Elias sent, save unto [a widow of Zarephath] . . . many lepers were in Israel in the time of Eliseus . . . and none of them was cleansed, save Naaman the Syrian" (Luke 4:25–27; cf. Isa. 65:1).

There was no *condition* in Naaman or the widow of Zarephath that might be described as "good," yet God saw fit to act in free grace toward them, even though both were heathen. He bypassed those who were actively engaged in "keeping the Law of Moses" and brought unmerited favor upon those who knew Him not.

Of course the inevitable happened when Jesus broached the subject of *unconditional election,* i.e., God's choosing to act in grace without some condition of good in His object. They tried to throw Him over a cliff to His death! Rebellious, sullen, bitter man, in his unregenerate state, hates any doctrine that refuses to give man at least part of the glory!

Take another example. When Jesus had finished His great discourse upon the fact that He is the "Bread come down from heaven," he said:

> "Therefore said I unto you that *no man can come to me, except* it were given unto him of my Father. From that

time many of his disciples went back, and walked no more with him" (John 6:65–66).

Why? Because the Son of God insisted that election is based upon the will of God and not the will of man! He deprived them of their ego-inflating notion that some *condition* of good existed in them that brought about their election.

If it were left up to man he would never believe, for man is totally depraved, totally incapable of that which is good. Left on his own to make a decision for Christ, without first being given life and faith by an act of God, man would never "come to Jesus."

"Ye *will not come* to me, that ye might have life" (John 5:40).

> 'Tis not that I did choose Thee.
> For, Lord, that could not be:
> This heart would still refuse Thee,
> Hadst Thou not chosen me!
>
> *Josiah Conder, 1836*

III

Limited
Atonement

We now come to what may well be the most difficult of the *Five Points of Calvinism* because the Christian community has been so emotionally conditioned by false practices rising out of false doctrine related to raising up missionaries and collecting funds for same.

When we speak of the meritorious work of Christ on the cross, do we rightfully say that He died for all men equally and alike (as say the Arminians), or do we more accurately state (with the Calvinists) that Christ died for the elect only?

Before jumping to a hasty conclusion, based on emotions and denominational traditions, let us see what the Word of God and continuing logic have to say about this vitally important matter.

Much of what we think about the atoning death of Christ will be tempered by what we understand the simple word *world* to mean. In the Gospel of John this word has special significance in that it may have any one of seven different meanings: (1) the classical sense, i.e., the *orderly* universe, (2) the earth itself, (3) the human inhabitants of earth, by metonomy, (4) mankind under the Creator's judgment, alienated from His life, in the ethical sense, (5) the public who were about Christ, Jews in particular, (6) the kingdom of evil forces, angelic as well as human, as related to the earth, and (7) men out of every tribe and nation but not all tribes and nations as a whole.

In other words the term *world* may refer to all that God has created, or to the earthen sphere upon which mankind dwells, or to mankind as a whole, or to the Palestinian contemporaries of our Lord, the Jew in particular, or to all evil forces related to the earth and in rebellion against God, or to persons selected out of every tribe and nation upon the face of the earth. Wherever the word appears it must be dealt with *in context* in much the same way that the word *all* must be examined. For example, the Scripture records the Pharisees as saying:

"Behold, the world is gone after him" (John 12:19).

Now it is obvious from the context that not all of humanity was following Jesus, for the speakers themselves refused to do so. Furthermore, we may be assured that not every human being on the face of the earth was following the Savior. On that occasion "the world" includes only those persons, whether Jew or Gentile, who were drawn enthusiastically to follow our Lord (for they had heard that He had raised Lazarus from the dead).

Take the golden text as an example:

"For God so loved the *world*, that he gave his only begotten Son, that whosoever believeth in him should not perish, but have everlasting life" (John 3:16).

The **Arminian** logically assumes that the word *world* means all of humanity because he believes in *postdestination* ("destiny determined *after* God foresees man's work of positive volition toward Christ"). The **Calvinist** logically assumes the definition of *world* to be "men out of every tribe and nation, but not all tribes and nations as a whole." This grows out of his conviction that Scripture teaches that election is based upon God's purpose, which is not affected by any *condition* on the part of man, since man's will is not free but bound by Satan, sin, and death.

You see, if you believe that the Bible teaches that God is sovereign, His plan immutable, and His election unconditional, you *must* conclude that the atonement is limited to those whom He freely willed to make the objects of grace. (Actually *grace* means unmerited favor. It is an act that is wholly undeserved, so that the term, by its very nature of definition, denies *conditional* election.) The Arminian view insists that it is man's act of faith that merits his being elected according to the foreknowledge of God. If such be the case man is saved by works and not by the grace of God, because he has done at least one thing pleasing to God, and all on his own! Paul understood this and affirmed that we are

"justified freely by *his grace* . . ." (Rom. 3:24).

To return briefly to John 3:16, let us ask the question, "For whom did Christ die?" *Backtrack* the verse with the questions:

1. Who is it that will not perish but have everlasting life?

47

2. Who is it that will believe, according to Scripture?
3. Who, then, is included in the word *world?*

Nearly everyone will agree that the answer to the first question is "whosoever believeth in Him." The **Arminian** will answer the second question, "Whoever, of his own *free will,* chooses to trust in Christ." The **Calvinist** will answer, "Those whom the Father chose in Christ, of His own free will." Now, note something amazing! Both are hereby agreed that the "world," in terms of those for whom Christ died, i.e., believers, means "men out of every tribe and nation, but not all tribes and nations as a whole," since not all will trust in Christ.

The **Arminian** must at least agree that although the blood of Christ is *sufficient* in value (since it is the "blood of God"), and His death is of *infinite* worth in the eyes of God, it is *efficient* or effectual only so far as the *elect* are concerned (whether the view be conditional or unconditional election). Actually the Arminian view of universal atonement is not tenable. His only *out* is to say that the will of God is foiled by man, because Christ supposedly died for all men whom God wanted to save but could not. This, of course, would mean that God is not omnipotent and that Christ gained only a small victory at the cross, since more men have died in unbelief than have gone to glory through faith in the Savior's finished work at Calvary. Someone will cry, Peter says:

> "The Lord is . . . not willing that any should perish" (2 Peter 3:9).

True, but let's be fair with the basic rules of English grammar and interpretation (or Greek, if you are able, since both come to the same conclusion). Begin by answering the question, "To whom is his second epistle, in which this statement is found, addressed?" Hear the apostle's own answer:

> "Simon Peter . . . to them that have obtained like precious faith with us through the righteousness of God and our Saviour Jesus Christ" (2 Peter 1:1).

He is writing to believers, to the elect, to those whose faith rests upon the righteousness of God and not on some *condition* of righteousness in and of themselves!

Next, ask the question, "What is the *context* of the passage in which the verse in question is found?" The answer is:

> "Where is the promise of his coming?" (2 Peter 3:4).

Then examine Peter's answer:

> "The Lord is not slack concerning his promise, as some men count slackness: but is longsuffering to us-ward . . ." (2 Peter 3:9).

Pause a moment and give a fair answer to the question, "To whom is Peter addressing himself when he uses the personal pronoun *us*?" Does he mean everyone, elect and lost alike, or is he writing

> "to them that have obtained like precious faith with *us*" (2 Peter 1:1)

as he says in the salutation of this epistle? The obvious answer is that Peter is speaking of believers *only* when he says "us."

Why is the Lord longsuffering regarding His promised coming? For the simple reason that He is "not willing that any [of US] should perish, but that all [of US] should come to repentance" (2 Peter 3:9).

Suppose that Jesus had raptured the church in 1850! Where would you be? You certainly would not have "believed on the Lord Jesus Christ" of *your own volition* unto salvation and a place in the church which is His bride!

No one can take 2 Peter 3:9 to support the *Arminian* position without wresting it out of context, misapplying it to the reprobate, and breaking basic rules for the interpretation of plain English or Greek. Peter's position there, as everywhere else, is that *Christ died for us* (the elect) and not for the whole world. He agrees with Paul who wrote:

"For (God) hath made (Christ) to be sin for *us* . . ."

and

"God commendeth His love toward *us,* in that, while we were yet sinners, *Christ died for us*" (2 Cor. 5:21; Rom. 5:8).

The only definition of the word *world,* as used in Scripture, that will fit every passage dealing with the salvation of the elect, is "men out of every tribe and nation, but not all mankind as a whole."

"If God be for *us,* who can be against us? He that spared not his own Son, but *delivered him up for us all,* how shall he not with him also *freely give us* all things? Who shall lay any thing to the charge of God's elect?" (Rom. 8:31–33).

Christ did not die for all men. Atonement was *limited!* Redemption was *particular!* Only the elect Bride of Christ was the object of His love. Paul says specifically:

> "Christ also *loved* the church, and *gave himself for* it [the church]" (Eph. 5:25).

The "all" for whom the Savior died are the elect whom the Father chose to give Him as a Bride "holy and without blemish." He did not elect us *because* we were holy and blameless! Paul says that God

> "hath *chosen us* in [Christ] before the foundation of the world, that we should be holy and without blame before him in love: Having predestinated us . . ." (Eph. 1:4).

Not chosen "because," but chosen "in order that" we might be holy and without blemish before God. We were *predestinated* "in love" because at no point in Scripture is the term "loved by God" applied to any persons other than the saints! It is never applied to the world at large, where the reprobate would be included. On the latter the "wrath of God" abides, while on the former "there is no condemnation." Only the *elect* are the specific objects of the love of God.

> ". . . Our Lord Jesus Christ . . . gave himself for *our* sins, that he might deliver *us* from this present evil world, *according to the will of God* and our Father: *To whom be glory* for ever and ever. Amen" (Gal. 1:3–5).

Take a very clear example of the fact that the Bible teaches *limited atonement.* In the tenth chapter of the Gospel of John our dear Lord identifies Himself as Jehovah, the "Good Shepherd" of Psalm 23. When He speaks of His "sheep" it is obvious that He is referring to those elect ones whom the Father gave Him for His own. He says:

> "I am the good shepherd, and know *my sheep,* and am known of *mine"* (John 10:14).

Who are His sheep who know Him and whom He knows? There can be no argument with the answer, *"His sheep* are the believers, the elect ones." Note the following statement:

> "I lay down my life for the sheep" (John 10:15).

In other words, when Christ gave His life on the cross of Calvary, He laid it down for His sheep, the elect ones of the Father! Not all men are included in that term "My sheep." Therefore Christ did not lay down His life for all men. To those standing around Him on that occasion, Jesus cries out:

> "Ye believe not, because ye are *not* of *my sheep,* as I said unto you" (John 10:26).

The reprobate, the non-elect, the unbeliever is not included in the number of those for whom Christ laid down His life. He died only for His sheep. Furthermore, when He calls them by name, they follow Him even as the Father predestinated that they should! Note His words:

> *"My sheep* hear *my* voice, and I know *them,* and *they* follow *me"* (John 10:27).

He *gives* eternal life as a free gift to those whom the Father *gave* Him before the universe was created! Salvation is the work of the irresistible, omnipotent God, the One who is "greater than all" others (angels and men included!).

> "My Father, which gave them me, is greater than all . . ." (John 10:29).

The Scriptures do not teach that Christ died to save everyone from his sins. We are told clearly that His death of deaths was designed for the salvation of His people, whom the Father chose in eternity past.

> "Ye are a *chosen* generation" (1 Peter 2:9).

Why does the **Calvinist** believe in limited atonement? For the simple reason that Christ and the holy apostles believed in it and taught it!

> "Thou shalt call his name JESUS: for he shall save *his people* from their sins" (Matt. 1:21).

God commends His love to us in that

> "while we were yet sinners, Christ died for us" (Rom. 5:8).

IV

Irresistible Grace

The fourth point of Calvinism counters the fourth point of Arminianism with "irresistible grace" versus "obstructable grace." The **Calvinist** insists that salvation is based on the free will of God, and since God is omnipotent, His grace cannot be resisted. The **Arminian** replies that salvation is based upon the free will of man, who is capable of rejecting the sovereign will of God (even when wooed by the Holy Spirit). He is powerful enough to obstruct or resist the grace of the God who desperately wants all men to be saved!

Perhaps we should best begin by defining the Greek word *charis* which is consistently translated *grace* in the New Testament. The basic meaning of the word is "unmerited favor." Grace is something that God does for man, which man does not merit—which he does not deserve by any stretch of the imagination. If man deserves what he gets from God, he has earned it. Works earn rewards, but he who has no works to *condition*

God's favor must cry out for grace. This is the basis for Paul's contention that

> "to him that *worketh* is the reward not reckoned of grace, but of debt. But to him that worketh *not,* but believeth on him that justifieth *the ungodly,* his faith is counted for righteousness" (Rom. 4:4–5).

Since *faith* is the "gift of God" and is "not of works," it is an act of grace (of "unmerited favor") on the part of God. If the *work* of *faith* is man's work then God is indebted to him. However, if *faith* is God's work and God's gift to man, then man possesses absolutely no condition in himself that merits salvation as a reward.

> "(God) hath saved *us* . . . not according to our works, but according to *his own purpose* and grace, which was given *us in Christ Jesus before the world began*" (2 Tim. 1:9).

What is meant when the Calvinist speaks of irresistible grace? We answer first in the negative. It does *not* mean that God does violence to man's spirit by forcing him to do something he does not want to do. (He did not force Judas to do what he did. Judas acted freely, according to the good pleasure of Satan his master, by doing what his dead human spirit, his sin-corrupted soul, dictated he should do. That is precisely why Christ, knowing whom He had chosen to be with Him day after day during his three and one-half years of public ministry, chose Judas.) Judas, without coercion, fulfilled the will of God (cf. Acts 2:22–23).

Irresistible, when used of the grace of God toward His elect, means that God, of His own free will, gives life to whom He chooses. Since the *living* human spirit, which is "born of God," finds the living God wholly *irresistible,* just as a *dead* human spirit finds the god of the dead (Satan) wholly irresistible, the Lord "quickens" ("makes alive") all whom He chose in Christ Jesus before the foundation of the world. It is the gift of the new nature that makes us find Jesus Christ absolutely irresistible. A hog, because of its very nature, loves to wallow in the muck and mire, while a lamb, because of its nature, disdains mud wallowing. "Dead in trespasses and sins," the unregenerate wallow in sin and unbelief because it is their nature to do so. Yet, when God gives His elect, who are the direct objects of His love, a "new nature," the old things pass away and all things become new! The new nature, which is a living human spirit, a new creation in Christ, finds God as irresistible as his formerly "dead" human spirit once found the devil irresistible.

The **Arminian,** however, insists that the omnipotent God can be obstructed in his will to save all men by the puny, impotent will of any individual. In other words the Holy Spirit Himself is rendered impotent to impart life, if it is the pleasure of the sinner to reject Christ and resist the drawing of the Spirit of God. This is contrary to the words of Jesus:

> "The Son quickeneth *whom he will . . .*" (John 5:21).

Nowhere does the Bible say that a man chooses eternal life of *his own will.* On the contrary Scripture states that whoever the Father gives to His dear Son *shall* come because it is *His will* that they come. Hear Jesus!

> "All that the Father giveth me *shall come* to me; and him that cometh to me I will in no wise cast out" (John 6:37).

Who is it that our Lord declares He will never "cast out"? According to His words, given in the first half of the sentence, it is those whom the Father has determined "shall come" to Him. Irresistible grace!

Be logical in your thinking about the matter of *will*. There is the *will of God*, concerning which the Bible says:

> "He doeth according to his *will* in the army of heaven, and among the inhabitants of the earth: and none can stay his hand . . ." (Dan. 4:35).

Next, we have the *will of Satan*, the most powerful creature that Jehovah ever created. As the arch enemy of God, and far more powerful than man, who was created "a little lower than the angels," Satan is, nevertheless, far less powerful than God. This is seen in that Jehovah puts strict limits on what He will allow the old Accuser of the Brethren to do. The record of Job gives a number of examples of the boundaries established by the Lord that Satan could not cross, as he persecuted Job. Therefore, even though Satan may well be more powerful than even the holy angels, he is not *omnipotent* like Jehovah. Neither is he *omniscient* nor omnipresent like Jehovah. He is a second-rate power.

Man is a third-rate power. He is not able to resist Satan because his will is inferior to the will of the devil. Paul says that the unregenerate, who "oppose" God's servants who teach the Word,

> "are taken captive by [the devil] at his will" (2 Tim. 2:26).

How can Satan ensnare the lost "at his will"? For the simple reason that man, without the Holy Spirit, is an inferior power who cannot resist the most powerful creature God ever made! This is why those who are still "dead in trespasses and sins" are governed by the counter-plan of the Evil One, walking "according to the course of this world, (walking) according to the prince of the power of the air, the spirit that now worketh in the children of disobedience . . ." (Eph. 2:2).

The reprobate are maneuvered by the devil. They will his will because they are children of wrath and under condemnation by God. The lost have "bound wills," for they are irresistibly *drawn* to the god of the dead *unless* the God of the living sees fit to give them the gift of life and faith.

The reprobate non-elect are never seen as the objects of the saving love of God. Only the elect, whom the Father willed to give to His Son as a bride, are ever spoken of as "beloved of the Lord." (Check your concordance, and see!)

I shall not weary you by pointing out that His love was not based on some fancied *condition* of "good" in us. (Paul says God loved us when we were still "dead in sins.") We were not saved because He foreknew of a *good work of faith* resulting from *our* positive volition toward Jesus. No, that would put God in debt to sinful man. Paul says it was "all of grace." Hallelujah!

"But God, who is rich in mercy, for *his great love* wherewith *he loved us,* even when we were dead in sins, hath *quickened us* [made us alive] together with Christ, (by grace ye are saved;)" (Eph. 2:4–5).

Even the **Arminian** must realize that when he claims that the grace of the God who *wills* that all men shall be saved can be resisted and rejected, he is stating that Jehovah is *not omnipotent.* He is claiming that man, a third-rate power, *under* the control of a higher second-rate power, has such fantastic "free will" that he can break the higher power of Satan to "choose" his way to heaven! Or is it that the heavenly Father is "permissive" and wills to *allow* the objects of His great love to go to hell if they so desire? Or is it that finite man can resist the first-rate power of Jehovah (the *Omnipotent* Creator) because he, the third-rate power, is greater than God? Unbelievable!

Man *cannot* come to Christ because man is bound by Satan. Man *will not* come because he finds Satan *irresistible* and Jehovah despicable. Man does not have a "free will," he has a devil-bound will. Man does not have the "power" to resist God should God "will" to save him. Man is not only third-rate as a power under the god of the dead, but he cannot even resist his bad habits and the lusts of the flesh! Man needs for God to *draw* him irresistibly by His grace, or man will never make so much as a single step in the direction of Christ. Hence the words of our Lord:

> "*No man can come* to me, except the Father which hath sent me *draw* him" (John 6:44).

A plain example of this is the businesswoman named Lydia who heard the apostles teaching the Word of God, and

> "whose heart the Lord opened . . ." (Acts 16:14).

Who opened her heart to Jesus? Does the Bible teach that the sinner opened her heart to the Lord, or does Scripture teach that it is the Lord who opens hearts?

Man is totally depraved, being devoid of any inclination to good. He never once has a *condition* in and of himself which *merits* salvation, therefore he is *unconditionally elected* to be the recipient of life and faith. Christ did *not* die for all men, but only for those whom the Father chose of His free will out of every nation and tribe upon the face of the earth. The death of Christ and His precious blood were designed specifically for those whom God determined *should come* to His dear Son in faith by means of His "irresistible grace," through the blessed Holy Spirit's gift of life.

V

Perseverance of the Saints

The Remonstrants **(Arminians)** taught that a saved person could "fall from grace," thereby losing the salvation he had once gained. Since the act of faith is *man's will* unto salvation, it stands to reason that if he fails to continue in faith, or commits some sin worthy of condemnation, then *by his own will* he may reject God and turn back to his old master. That, of course, is the only logical conclusion that can be reached if one holds the first four points of Arminianism, and the brilliant students of Arminius knew it.

The **Calvinists** taught that the saints, otherwise known as the "elect," can never be lost since their salvation is by the will of the unchanging, omnipotent God. Since no *condition* in man determines his being chosen, because Scripture teaches *unconditional election*, it stands to reason that there is nothing he can do to get himself "unsaved" once he has been saved by God's grace. Surely, reasons the Calvinist, if it is the *will of God*

63

that I am saved, and since He "changes not," then I begin my salvation, continue my salvation, and enter heaven a *saved* person because He has *willed* it so!

"Of *his own will* begat he *us* with the word of truth" (James 1:18).

Thus we have two diametrically opposed positions. One is an opinion, based on the reasoning of the carnal mind (which is ever at enmity with God), and the other is a fact based upon Scripture. Let us, therefore, look at what the Bible says.

Paul takes up this blessed subject by assuring the believers at Philippi:

"Being confident of this very thing, that he that hath begun a good work in you will perform it until the day of Jesus Christ" (Phil. 1:6).

The God who is the Author of the "good work" (which He, not man, began in His elect) will "perform it" (continuous tense, or "keep on performing" the good work in the saint) until the "day of Jesus Christ," when we shall receive sinless, resurrection bodies! Again, that "good work" will also be His work and not ours! Hence Paul's other words to the Philippian believers:

"Our [citizenship] is in heaven; from whence also we look for the Saviour, the Lord Jesus Christ: who shall change our vile body, that it may be fashioned like unto his glorious body, according to the working whereby he is able even to subdue all things unto himself" (Phil. 3:20–21).

Notice to whom the Father has given "all power" so that "He is able to subdue *all things* to Himself." It is our coming Savior-King! It is the glorious One of whom Scripture says:

> "Thou hast given him *power over all flesh,* that he [Christ] should give eternal life to *as many as thou hast given him*" (John 17:2).

How many? Who? The blessed Son of God also stated in the plainest of terms,

> "This is the *Father's will which hath* sent me, that of all which he hath given me *I shall lose nothing,* but should raise it up again at the last day" (John 6:39).

What does your Bible say? Will "some" given to the Son be lost, or will "none" be lost? Since salvation is of the Lord, it is evident that once we are saved by the power of God, we are always saved. We had absolutely nothing to do with "getting saved," and we have absolutely nothing to do with "keeping saved," because salvation is by the grace of God and not the vascillating will of man! Notice the words of God the Son:

> "I give unto them [His sheep] *eternal* life; and they shall *never* perish, neither shall any man pluck them out of my hand" (John 10:28).

How long is the salvation that God gives His own? Will the elect sheep of the Good Shepherd ever *perish?* Whose word do we take? Man's or God's? Why is it that some will take unclear passages of Scripture to attempt to nullify the superclear passages? Can it be because they will not have salvation by God's sovereign grace, but will either have salvation by their own work of faith or none at all?

Take the words of Peter, as he was directed and controlled by the Holy Spirit, who wrote that the elect are destined

> "to an inheritance *incorruptible,* and undefiled, and that fadeth not away, reserved in heaven for you, who are *kept by the power of God* through faith unto salvation ready to be revealed in the last time" (1 Peter 1:4–5).

No wonder Paul so exultantly sings:

> "I know whom I have believed, and am persuaded that *he is able to keep* that which I have committed unto him against that day" (2 Tim. 1:12; cf. John 17:11).

We are predestined unto heaven because God has elected us to glory. This is why the Thessalonians are assured:

> "He called you . . . to the obtaining of the glory" (2 Thess. 2:14).

Heaven is our home. The glory of that heavenly dwelling is our *inheritance* because God has freely willed it so by His grace!

> "In [Christ] we have obtained an *inheritance,* being *predestinated* according to the *purpose* of him who worketh *all* things after the counsel of *his own will*" (Eph. 1:11).

> "The election hath obtained it, and the rest were blinded" (Rom. 11:7).

> "We are bound to give thanks always to God for you, brethren *beloved of the Lord,* because God hath from the beginning chosen you to salvation" (2 Thess. 2:13).

Small wonder that Paul, knowing that the omnipotent Creator had made him the object of eternal love, should be able to say boldly:

> "The Lord shall deliver me from every evil work, and will *preserve* me unto his heavenly kingdom . . ." (2 Tim. 4:18).

Small wonder that Jude should write to the elect of God,

> "to them that are sanctified by God the Father, and *preserved* in Jesus Christ, and called" (Jude 1).

Small wonder that Paul confidently prays for the elect saints at Thessalonica:

> "And the very God of peace sanctify you wholly; and I pray God your whole spirit and soul and body be *preserved* blameless unto the coming of our Lord Jesus Christ. Faithful is he that calleth you, who also will do it" (1 Thess. 5:23–24).

Who is it that *preserves* the believer "blameless" until He comes for us? Who is it that is faithful? Who is it that will do this marvelous work of sanctifying and keeping? Why, "our Lord Jesus Christ", of course! The saints persevere because He perseveres! We are not kept in small pieces either. We are kept as a complete "spirit and soul and body"!

Or, as Jude says in the beautiful doxology at the end of his forceful epistle:

> "Now unto him who is *able to keep you from falling,* and to present you faultless before the presence of his glory with exceeding joy, to the only wise God our Saviour, be glory and majesty, dominion and power, both now and ever" (Jude 24–25).

67

Yes, the saints will "persevere" because the Savior declares that He will persevere on their behalf. He will keep them. If perseverance depended upon fickle man with his fallen sin nature, he would be hopeless. *Perseverance of the saints* is dependent upon *irresistible grace*, granted us because Christ died for us since the atonement we have by His blood was *limited* to the elect. That election, praise the Lord, was not based upon some *condition* of good foreknown to be in us since "there is none good, no not one." By the grace of God it was an *unconditional election* because no condition could be found! No condition could be found because man is *totally depraved*, i.e., totally incapable of exercising good will toward God, wholly impotent to call himself to life or to free himself from the superhuman power of the god of the dead.

In Conclusion

At this point the author of this evaluation of the *Five Points of Arminianism* and the *Five Points of Calvinism*, in the light of Scripture, must make a confession. Not many years ago I was of **Arminian** persuasion. I was born again by the will and grace of God at a Methodist altar. I later became a Methodist minister. As I sought to prepare expository messages for my people I researched the meaning of every key word in the Greek or Hebrew. The result was that I soon found that the doctrinal position of my denomination was not compatible with that of the Bible. Finally the day came that I courteously resigned my pulpit. I had no grudge with the church, or with the Bishop, for I had always been well favored during my nine years of service. I simply felt that it was not right for me to teach contrary to the organization I served. My exodus was such that the Bishop returned my ordination papers to me with words of commendation for services faithfully rendered, and I was on my way on the most exciting adventure by faith I had had until then.

Continuing my research of the Scriptures, reading reference works avidly, and perusing volume after volume of church history (particularly that of the Protestant Reformation), I began to see the great gulf between modern theology and the Word of God. This great gulf was made most apparent to my heart by the Spirit of God when I began to analyze the differences between what is historically known as **Arminianism** and **Calvinism.** Like many preachers and laymen I had heard both words used as evil terms to condemn those of opposite persuasion, but I had never really known who believed what. This little booklet is the result of much searching of the Scriptures to "see if these things be so." It has not been written so much with the desire to contradict **Arminianism,** although it does that, as to show that the doctrines of the Reformers (known as **Calvinism**), are more nearly that of Holy Scripture than any other system of theology with which I am familiar.

I have already learned that he who takes the doctrinal position of the great Reformers will become the object of derision on the part of those whose theology is based upon the emotions, denominational traditions and doctrines, and human reasoning, yet I cannot leave what I am convinced is the position of Christ and His apostles. With Luther I must cry, "I am captive of the Word of God! I can do no other! Here I stand!"

Yet, even as I stand in assurance that Reformation doctrine is Bible doctrine, I stand humbly aware that not too many years ago I was of Arminian persuasion, therefore I do not condemn those who disagree with my present position. I only pray that the Holy Spirit will illumine each of our hearts so that we might love one another with the heavenly Agape with which He loves us (in spite of ourselves) and grow together in the knowledge of Truth.

Perhaps the words of Charles Haddon Spurgeon can best express my feelings in this small work on T-U-L-I-P.

"We believe in the five great points commonly known as
Calvinistic; but we do not regard these five points as
being barbed shafts which we are to thrust between the
ribs of our fellow-Christians. We look upon them as
being five great lamps which help to irradiate the cross;
or, rather, five bright emanations springing from the
glorious covenant of our Triune God, and illustrating
the great doctrine of Jesus crucified."

I sought the Lord, and afterward I knew
He moved my soul to seek Him seeking me;
It was not I that found, O Saviour true,
No, I was found of Thee.

Thou didst reach forth Thy hand and mine enfold;
I walked and sank not on the storm-vexed sea;
'Twas not so much that I on Thee took hold,
As Thou, dear Lord, on me.

I find, I walk, I love, but, O the whole
Of love is but my answer, Lord, to Thee!
For Thou wert long beforehand with my soul,
Always Thou lovedst me.

Anon., c. 1878

Selections from the Westminster Confession of Faith (1648)

CHAPTER III
Of God's Eternal Decree

I   God, from all eternity, did, by the most wise and holy counsel of His own will, freely, and unchangeably ordain whatsoever comes to pass: yet so, as thereby neither is God the author of sin, nor is violence offered to the will of the creatures; nor is the liberty or contingency of second causes taken away, but rather established.

II   Although God knows whatsoever may or can come to pass on all supposed conditions, yet He has not decreed anything because He foresaw it as future, or as that which would come to pass on such conditions.

III   By the decree of God, for the manifestation of His glory, some men and angels are predestinated to everlasting life; and others foreordained to everlasting death.

IV   These angels and men, thus predestinated and foreordained, are particularly and unchangeably designed, and their number so certain and definite that it cannot be either increased or diminished.

V   Those of mankind that are predestinated to life, God, before the foundation of the world was laid, according to His eternal and immutable purpose, and the secret counsel and good pleasure of His will, has chosen, in Christ, to everlasting glory, out of His mere free grace and love, without any foresight of faith, or good works, or perseverance in either of them, or any other thing in the creature, as conditions, or causes moving Him thereunto; and all to the praise of His glorious grace.

VI   As God has appointed the elect to glory, so has He, by the eternal and most free purpose of His will, foreordained all the means thereunto. Wherefore, they who are elected, being fallen in Adam, are redeemed by Christ, are effectually called to faith in Christ by His Spirit working in due season, are justified, adopted, sanctified, and kept by His power, through faith, to salvation. Neither are any other redeemed by Christ, effectually called, justified, adopted, sanctified, and saved, but the elect only.

VII   The rest of mankind God was pleased, according to the unsearchable counsel of His own will, whereby He extends or withholds mercy, as He pleases, for the glory of His sovereign power over His creatures, to pass by; and to ordain them to dishonor and wrath for their sin, to the praise of His glorious justice.

VIII   The doctrine of this high mystery of pre-destination is to be handled with special prudence and care, that men, attending the will of God revealed in His Word, and yielding obedience thereunto, may, from the certainty of their effectual vocation, be assured of their eternal election. So shall this doctrine afford matter of praise, reverence, and admiration of God; and of humility, diligence, and abundant consolation to all that sincerely obey the Gospel.

CHAPTER V
Of Providence

I   God the great Creator of all things does uphold, direct, dispose, and govern all creatures, actions, and things, from the greatest even to the least, by His most wise and holy providence, according to His infallible foreknowledge, and the free and immutable counsel of His own will, to the praise of the glory of His wisdom, power, justice, goodness, and mercy.

II   Although, in relation to the foreknowledge and decree of God, the first Cause, all things come to pass immutably and infallibly; yet, by the same providence He orders them to fall out according to the nature of second causes, either necessarily, freely, or contingently.

III   God, in His ordinary providence, makes use of means, yet is free to work without, above, and against them, at His pleasure.

IV   The almighty power, unsearchable wisdom, and infinite goodness of God so far manifest themselves in His providence, that it extends itself to the first fall, and all other sins of angels and men; and that not by a bare permission, but such as has joined with it a most wise and powerful bounding, and otherwise ordering, and governing of them in a manifold dispensation, to His own holy ends; yet so, as the sinfulness thereof proceeds only from the creature, and not from God, who, being most holy and righteous, neither is nor can be the author or approver of sin.

V   The most wise, righteous, and gracious God does oftentimes leave for a season His own children to manifold temptations and the corruption of their own hearts, to chastise them for their former sins, or to discover to them the hidden strength of corruption and deceitfulness of their hearts, that they may be humbled; and to raise them to a more close and constant dependence for their support upon Himself, and to make them more watchful against all future occasions of sin, and for sundry other just and holy ends.

VI   As for those wicked and ungodly men whom God, as a righteous Judge, for former sins, does blind and harden, from them He not only withholds His grace whereby they might have been enlightened in their understandings, and wrought upon in their hearts; but sometimes also withdraws the gifts which they had, and exposes them to such objects as their corruption makes occasions of sin; and, withal, gives them over to their own lusts, the temptations of the world, and the power of Satan, whereby it comes to pass that they harden themselves, even under those means which God uses for the softening of others.

CHAPTER VII
Of God's Covenant with Man

II   The first covenant made with man was a covenant of works, wherein life was promised to Adam; and in him to his posterity, upon condition of perfect and personal obedience.

III   Man, by his fall, having made himself uncapable of life by that covenant, the Lord was pleased to make a second, commonly called the covenant of grace; wherein He freely offers to sinners life and salvation by Jesus Christ; requiring of them faith in Him, that they may be saved, and promising to give *to all those that are ordained to eternal life* His Holy Spirit, to make them willing, and able to believe.

CHAPTER VIII
Of Christ the Mediator

I   It pleased God, in His eternal purpose, to choose and ordain the Lord Jesus, His only begotten Son, to be the Mediator between God and man, the Prophet, Priest, and King, the Head and Savior of His Church, the Heir of all things, and Judge of the world: to whom He did from all eternity give a people, to be His seed, and to be by Him in time redeemed, called, justified, sanctified, and glorified.

V   The Lord Jesus, by His perfect obedience, and sacrifice of Himself, which He, through the eternal Spirit, once offered up to God, has fully satisfied the justice of His Father; and purchased, not only reconciliation, but an everlasting inheritance in the kingdom of heaven, for all those whom the Father has given to Him.

VIII   To all those for whom Christ has purchased redemption, He does certainly and effectually apply and communicate the same; making intercession for them and revealing to them, in and by the Word, the mysteries of salvation; effectually persuading them by His Spirit to believe and obey, and governing their hearts by His Word and Spirit; overcoming all their enemies by His almighty power and wisdom, in such manner and ways, as are most consonant to His wonderful and unsearchable dispensation.

CHAPTER IX
Of Free-Will

I   God has endued the will of man with that natural liberty, that it is neither forced, nor, by any absolute necessity of nature, determined to good, or evil.

II   Man, in his state of innocency, had freedom and power to will and to do that which was good and well pleasing to God; but yet, mutably, so that he might fall from it.

III   Man, by his fall into a state of sin, has wholly lost all ability of will to any spiritual good accompanying salvation: so as, a natural man, being altogether averse from that good, and dead in sin, is not able by his own strength to convert himself, or to prepare himself thereunto.

IV   When God converts a sinner and translates him into the state of grace, He frees him from his natural bondage under sin; and, by His grace alone, enables him freely to will and to do that which is spiritually good; yet so, as that by reason of his remaining corruption, he does not perfectly, nor only, will that which is good, but does also will that which is evil.

V   The will of man is made perfectly and immutably free to good alone in the state of glory only.

CHAPTER X
Of Effectual Calling

I   All those whom God has predestinated to life, and those only, He is pleased, in His appointed and accepted time, effectually to call, by His Word and Spirit, out of that state of sin and death, in which they are by nature, to grace and salvation, by Jesus Christ; enlightening their minds spiritually and savingly to understand the things of God, taking away their heart of stone, and giving to them a heart of flesh; renewing their wills, and by His almighty power determining them to that which is good, and effectually drawing them to Jesus Christ; yet so, as they come most freely, being made willing by His grace.

II   This effectual call is of God's free and special grace alone, not from anything at all foreseen in man, who is altogether passive therein, until, being made alive and renewed by the Holy Spirit, he is thereby enabled to answer this call, and to embrace the grace offered and conveyed in it.

Historical Background

The chart that begins on page 82 is designed for use with the book TULIP. The title of the book is gained from an old acrostic formed by the initial letters of the *Five Points of Calvinism,* namely: **T**otal depravity, **U**nconditional election, **L**imited atonement, **I**rresistible grace, and **P**erseverance of the saints.

These five points or doctrinal positions were formulated by the Great Synod of Dort in reply to a document called "Remonstrance." This "protest" was presented to the State of Holland by the disciples of a Dutch seminary professor (Jacob Hermann) whose Latin surname was *Arminius.* Arminius (1560–1609) was only four years old when the great Reformer, John Calvin (1509–1564) died. Although reared in the Reformed tradition, Arminius had serious doubts as to the sovereign grace of God, for his natural reason was sympathetic to the teachings of Pelagius and Erasmus concerning the free will of man. Within a year of the death of Arminius, his disciples formulated his teachings into five main points, which they proceeded to present to the State with the desire that the *Belgic Confession* and *Heidelberg Catechism* be replaced by the teachings of their professor.

The great Synod of Dort was convened by the States-General in 1618 for the specific purpose of examining the *Five Points of Arminianism* in the light of Holy Scripture. 84 theologians and 18 secular commissioners were assembled for 154 sessions lasting from November 13, 1618, until May 9, 1619. After thorough examination of the doctrines of Arminius, carefully comparing his teachings with those of Holy Writ, the Synod determined that his views were *heretical.* The members of the Great Synod did not stop there, however, but carefully formulated a five-point rebuttal from the Scriptures, which later became known as the *Five Points of Calvinism.*

History reveals that neither "Arminianism" nor "Calvinism" is *new.* A fifth-century heretic by the name of Pelagius, who denied that the human nature was corrupted by sin, had taught that man possessed absolute "free will" whereby he could either choose or reject God. His historic opponent was the great theologian, Augustine, who insisted that the Scriptures taught that man was dead in trespasses and sins and in bondage to Satan. Man's will, said Augustine, was not in the least "free."

During the Protestant Reformation the issue was sharpened. Erasmus, the brilliant humanist and theologian of the Church of Rome, issued a "Diatribe" in which he protested sovereign grace and argued for man's free will to "make a decision" for Christ. This was countered by the volatile pen of the great Protestant Reformer, Martin Luther, in his thesis on "The Bondage of the Human Will." (The book is available in an excellent English translation.)

Arminianism is but a refinement of Pelagianism and the sophisticated reasoning of Erasmus. Later popularized by the Wesley brothers in England with great effect, Arminianism has come down into the twentieth century as the basis for modern *evangelism of the masses.*

The purpose of this chart is to assist the student in defining the real issues at stake. It simply states the basic ideas of the five points of both the Arminian and the Calvinist and lists the Scriptures used by each party in support of its views, with a brief commentary as to the weaknesses of the former system.

Point
_____

THE ARMINIAN VIEW   "Free Will"
_____

Man's depravity, as a result of the fall, is not total but partial. Man has not lost the faculty of self-determination, nor the ability to freely will that which is good in the sight of God. Man is the author of repentance and faith unto salvation since the human will is viewed by the Arminian as one of the causes of regeneration, if man freely wills to cooperate with the Holy Spirit.

John 3:16—"For God so loved the world, that he gave his only begotten Son, that whosoever believeth in him should not perish, but have everlasting life."
Acts 2:38—"Repent, and be baptized, every one of you in the name of Jesus Christ for the remission of sins."
Acts 16:31—"Believe on the Lord Jesus Christ, and thou shalt be saved, and thy house."
Romans 10:9—"If thou shalt confess with thy mouth the Lord Jesus, and shalt believe in thine heart that God hath raised him from the dead, thou shalt be saved."
1 John 3:23—"This is his commandment, That we should believe on the name of his Son Jesus Christ."
***"Whosoever will may come" is not to be found in the Bible.

"FREE WILL" OR "ACCOUNTABILITY"?

The careful observer will note that the Scriptures selected by the *Arminianist* in support of "free will" do not deal with that subject, but, rather, with man's *responsibility* to believe God and his *accountability* if he does not. There are two reasons for this: (1) There are no Scriptures that teach that man has a "free will," and (2) Arminius reasoned (contrary to Scripture) that "God has no right to hold man accountable to believe, nor condemn him for unbelief, if his will is not free to do so."

This is like saying that a kleptomaniac should not be held responsible for stealing, nor punished when caught, because he cannot help himself! It is the perverted view that says that a sex maniac should not be held responsible for rape or child molesting, nor punished for same, because he cannot control himself! (This may be the position of some "do-gooders," but it is not God's!) "Every one of us shall *give account* of himself to God," and those who reject His Word will be eternally punished in the Lake of Fire burning with brimstone.

The Scriptures teach that there is sufficient *light* given all men that, should they have the slightest inclination to come to the Light, they will be saved. The fact is that man is so infatuated with sin and unbelief, and so irresistibly drawn to Satan, that he loves darkness and hates the light (cf. John 1:9; 3:19; Rom. 1:18–20). Man is *responsible* to obey the Word of God and *accountable* when he refuses.

One

"Total Depravity"   THE CALVINIST VIEW

Man's depravity, as a result of the fall, is total. He does not possess *free will* because he is bound to Satan who takes man captive at his will. All people are born into this world spiritually dead in trespasses and sins so that their dead human spirits are irresistibly drawn to the god of the dead. Man is depraved in the sense that he is dead, blind, deaf, unteachable in the things of God and ruled by Satan through his perverse heart and corrupt soul.

TOTAL DEPRAVITY REACHES ALL MANKIND

Romans 5:12—"By one man (Adam) sin entered into the world, and death by sin; and so death passed upon all men, for that all have sinned."
Jeremiah 17:9—"The heart is *deceitful* above all things, and desperately *wicked.*"
Romans 3:11—"There is *none* that seeketh after God."
Proverbs 20:9—"Who can say, *I have made* my heart clean?"

BORN SPIRITUALLY DEAD

Psalm 58:3—"The wicked are estranged *from the womb:* They go astray as soon as they be born, speaking lies."
Psalm 51:5—"Behold, *I was shapen* in iniquity . . ."
John 3:3—"Except a man be born again, *he cannot see* the kingdom of God."
Genesis 8:21—". . . the imagination of man's heart is evil from his youth."
Ephesians 5:8—"Ye were sometimes darkness, but now are ye light in the Lord."

TAKEN CAPTIVE AT SATAN'S WILL

2 Timothy 2:25–26—". . . if God *peradventure will give them repentance* to the acknowledging of the truth; and that they may recover themselves out of the snare of the devil, who are *taken captive by him at his will.*"
John 8:44—"Ye are of your father the devil."

IRRESISTIBLY DRAWN TO SATAN

John 3:19—". . . men *loved darkness* rather than light."
Ephesians 2:1–3—"You . . . were dead in trespasses and sins; wherein in time past ye walked according to the course of this world, *according to the prince of the power of the air,* the spirit that now worketh in the children of disobedience; among whom also we all had our conversation in times past in the lusts of our flesh, fulfilling the desires of the flesh and of the mind; and *were by nature the children of wrath,* even as others."

DEPRAVED MAN SPIRITUALLY UNTEACHABLE

1 Corinthians 2:14—"The natural [soulish] *man receiveth not the things of the Spirit of God:* for they are foolishness unto him: neither can he know them, because they are spiritually discerned."

Point

THE ARMINIAN VIEW   "Conditional Election"

Election is *conditioned* upon man's good works of repentance and faith in Christ. If this is true, then election is based upon God's foreknowledge of who will respond to the offer of the gospel and freely will to exercise his faculty of self-determination and be saved. Man's good works of repentance and faith must *precede* God's good work of regeneration. He must "make a decision for Christ" and "let Jesus come into his heart," for God will not violate the will of man by giving life or opening the heart without man's permission.

1 Peter 1:2—"Elect *according to the foreknowledge of God* the Father . . ."
Romans 11:2—"God hath not cast away his people [Israel] *which he foreknew* . . ."
Proverbs 3:5—"*Trust in the LORD* with all thine heart; and lean not unto thine own understanding."
Mark 1:15—"*Repent* ye, and *believe* the gospel."
Mark 11:22—"And Jesus answering saith unto them, *Have faith* in God."
Matthew 8:13—"As thou hast believed, so be it done unto thee."
John 5:24—"Verily, verily, I say unto you, He that heareth my word, and believeth on him that sent me, hath everlasting life, and shall not come into condemnation; but is passed from death unto life."

"WHO ACTS FIRST?"

The Arminian believes that the human will is one of the *causes* of regeneration (synergism). This is why he believes that *election* is based on the *foreknowledge* of God who foresaw "who would believe" in eternity past. Foreknowing those who would freely will to *repent* of their sins and make a decision to place their *faith* in Christ, God *elected* them to salvation. This means that *repentance* and *faith* are man's "good works" whereby he establishes the *condition* for his being elected to be saved. *Arminianism* is a "works religion" at least to the extent that *man* must accomplish the good works of repentance and faith, with only the general assistance of the Holy Spirit, given all people alike.

The Calvinist believes that God alone is the cause of regeneration. Knowing that no man can or will establish any *condition* that can serve as a basis for his election, he follows the Scriptural position that declares that "foreknowledge" is grounded in the "purpose" of God to elect some to salvation without good works on their part. Every work that is related to salvation is God's work, for He alone can regenerate, open blind eyes, unstop deaf ears, evoke faith in Jesus Christ, illumine the dark recesses of a person's heart, and grant true repentance of sins by establishing a desire for purity in doctrine and life. *Calvinism* is strictly a "not of works, lest any man should boast" religion (Eph. 2:8–9) because it insists on giving God all the glory for all that is good.

Two

"Unconditional Election"   CALVINIST VIEW

Election is grounded entirely in the free will of God and in His purpose for those whom He chose "in Christ Jesus" before the foundation of the world. His fore-knowledge is based upon His purpose, for His purpose is the manifestation of His sovereign will. Since man is incapable of giving himself life, opening his own eyes, or teaching himself spiritual truth, God must elect to act on man's behalf. The work of regeneration, therefore, must precede faith and repentance and is the work of God. He must "open the heart" and cause His elect "to will and do" that which is pleasing to Him, otherwise none would believe.

GOD CHOOSES, NOT MAN

John 15:16—"Ye have *not* chosen me, but I have chosen you."
Acts 13:48—"*As many as were ordained* to eternal life believed."
Psalm 65:4—"Blessed is the man whom *Thou choosest, and causest to approach unto thee,* that he may dwell in thy courts."
Philippians 2:13—"It is *God* which worketh in you both to *will* and to do of his good pleasure."

ELECTION BASED ON GOD'S PURPOSE (PLAN)

Ephesians 1:11—". . . predestinated *according to the purpose* of him who wor-keth all things after the counsel of his own will."
2 Timothy 1:9—"[God] hath saved us, and called us with an holy calling, not according to our works, but *according to his own purpose and grace,* which was given us in Christ Jesus before the world began."

FOREKNOWLEDGE BASED ON GOD'S PURPOSE

Romans 8:28—"We know that all things work together for good to them that love God, to them who are *the called [ones] according to his purpose.* For whom he did foreknow, he also did predestinate . . ."

MAN IS INCAPABLE, GOD MUST INITIATE

John 6:44—"No man can come to me, except the Father . . . draw him."
Matthew 11:27—". . . no man knoweth . . . the Father, save the Son, and he to whomsoever the Son will *reveal* him."
Hebrews 12:2—"Jesus the *author* and finisher of our faith."
Acts 16:14—"Lydia . . . *whose heart the Lord opened,* that she attended unto the things which were spoken of Paul."
Luke 17:5—"And the apostles said unto the Lord, Increase our faith."

GOD'S WILL SHALL BE ACCOMPLISHED

Isaiah 55:11—"So shall my word be that goeth forth out of my mouth: it shall not return unto me void, but it shall accomplish that which I please, and it shall prosper in the thing whereto I sent it."

Point

THE ARMINIAN VIEW   "Universal Atonement"

Atonement is universal, since God loves all persons equally and alike, and Christ died for all persons, indiscriminately. The blood of Christ makes atonement for sin in the sense that it is the basis for offering pardon, but it does not accomplish pardon unless man freely wills to accept pardon. (Atonement is a term that is used broadly to include redemption, remission, propitiation, reconciliation, and all else accomplished by Christ on the cross.) The Arminian insists that it was accomplished for all mankind, indiscriminately.

John 3:16—"For God so loved the *world* that he gave his only begotten Son, that whosoever believeth in him should not perish, but have everlasting life."
2 Peter 3:9—"The Lord . . . is longsuffering to us-ward, not willing that any [person] should perish, but that all [persons] should come to repentance."
John 6:37—"All that the Father giveth me shall come to me; and *him that cometh to me* I will in no wise cast out."
John 1:29—"Behold the Lamb of God, which taketh away *the sin of the world.*"
Acts 10:43—"To [Christ] give all the prophets witness, that through his name whosoever believeth in him shall receive remission of sins."
John 1:12—"As many as received him, to them gave he power to become the sons of God, *even to them that believe on his name.*"

"GOD WANTS TO SAVE EVERYBODY!"

One of the most popular misrepresentations of God in modern evangelism is that "God loves everyone, and wants to save everybody." The first obvious thing about this fallacy is that the Holy Scriptures very clearly teach that there are many whom God hates! For example:

"It is written, Jacob have I loved, but Esau have I hated" (Rom. 9:13).

All who have any real working knowledge of the Bible know that if the Lord loves everyone and *really* wants to save all, He (as the omnipotent God who cannot be resisted) will do just that. The fact is, as Scripture abundantly illustrates, God neither loves all people equally and alike, nor is He going to save all.

Ask yourself such questions as "Who is it that will never perish, in John 3:16?" (Answer: "whosoever believeth in Him.") Question: Who are these believers? (Answer: the elect.) Question: Who, then, are the *real* objects of God's saving love in the "world," since only certain persons will be saved?" (Answer: elect believers. Certainly not all people!)

If you think of 2 Peter 3:9 and the phrase "not willing that any should perish," ask yourself, "To whom is Peter writing?" "To whom does 'US' refer in the verse?" If the *understood* personal pronoun is "US," then good grammar dictates that Peter is saying that God is *"not willing that any of US (believers) should perish."*

Three

"Limited Atonement"   THE CALVINIST VIEW

Atonement is for the elect only, since Christ died only for those whom the Father gave Him to be His Bride. Only the saints or elect ones are ever said to be "beloved of God," for they alone are the objects of His saving grace. The Calvinist reasons that if Christ died for all, then all will be saved. If only the elect are to be saved, then Christ died for them, and them alone. Although it is true that the blood of Christ is surely *sufficient* in value to atone for all, still it is obviously *efficient* only for those who are saved by His unmerited favor.

CHRIST'S DEATH ONLY FOR THE ELECT

John 10:14–15—"I . . . know my sheep, and am known of mine . . . and *I lay down my life for the sheep.*"
Romans 5:8—"God commendeth his love toward us, in that, while we were yet sinners, Christ died for us."
Galatians 1:3–4—"Our Lord Jesus Christ . . . gave himself for our sins, that *he might deliver* us from this present evil world, *according to the* will of God our Father."
Romans 8:32—"He that spared not his own Son, but *delivered him up for us all,* how shall he not with him also freely give us all things? Who shall lay any thing to the charge of God's elect?"
Ephesians 5:25—"Christ also loved the church, and *gave himself for it* [the church]."

CHRIST PRAYS ONLY FOR ELECT

John 17:9—"I pray for them [the elect]: I pray not for the world, but for *them whom thou hast given me* . . ."

THUS, ONLY ELECT ARE SAVED

Matthew 1:21—"He shall save *his people* from their sins."
2 Peter 3:9—"The Lord . . . is longsuffering to us-ward, not willing that any (of US) should perish, but that all (of US) should come to repentance."
Colossians 1:12–14—"Giving thanks unto *the Father, which hath made us meet to be partakers* of the inheritance of the saints in light: *Who hath delivered* us from the power of darkness, and *hath translated us* into the kingdom of his dear Son: In whom we have redemption through his blood, even the forgiveness of sins."
2 Thessalonians 2:13—"But we are bound to give thanks alway to God for you, *brethren beloved of the Lord,* because God hath from the beginning chosen you to salvation through sanctification of the Spirit and belief of the truth."

ONLY ELECT ARE BELOVED

1 Thessalonians 1:4—"Knowing brethren beloved, your election of God."
Colossians 3:12—". . . the elect of God, holy and beloved."

Point

THE ARMINIAN VIEW   "Obstructable Grace"

It is the will of God that all should be saved, but His will can be resisted since each person has the faculty of self-determination. Since God loves all people, indiscriminately, He woos them with His Holy Spirit, seeking to draw them to faith in Christ. The external call of the gospel is accompanied by universal sufficient grace, but it will not be found irresistible to all men, but is obstructable by man's "free will."

John 1:12—"But *as many as received him,* to them gave he power to become the sons of God, even to them that believe on his name."
John 3:36—"He that believeth on the Son hath everlasting life: and he that believeth not the Son shall not see life; but the wrath of God abideth on him."
John 3:18–21—"He that believeth on him is not condemned: but he that believeth not is condemned already, because he hath not believed in the name of the only begotten Son of God. And this is the condemnation, that light is come into the world, and men loved darkness rather than light, because their deeds were evil. For every one that doeth evil hateth the light, neither cometh to the light, lest his deeds should be reproved. But he that doeth truth cometh to the light, that his deeds may be made manifest, that they are wrought in God."
John 5:40—"Ye *will not come* to me . . ."
John 8:45—"Because I tell you the truth, ye believe me not."

WHO IS "IRRESISTIBLE" AND WHY

One of the wildest ideas so prevalent among mission-minded people is that the lost are longing to hear the gospel and hungry for the things of God! Anyone who finds everyone eager to believe on the Lord Jesus Christ needs to be apprised of the fact that the "Jesus" he is offering, and the "word" he is sharing, are not of God. Our Lord is very clear in His teaching that the world hates Him, His Word, and His messengers (cf. John 15:15 and following).

"Irresistibility" is the reason for the world hating God and His elect. Satan is the god of all dead spirits, angelic and human. Just as dirty-minded men seek companionship of others with vile thoughts, and those with pure minds delight in the companionship of likeminded persons, so dead human spirits are irresistibly drawn to the leader of the spiritually dead. (This is why no unregenerate person ever freely "wills" to turn to God. The dead human spirit is repelled by the God of living spirits, both human and angelic.)

However, for the very same reason, all living spirits find the God of the living "irresistible." They cannot help being drawn to Him, trusting Him, loving Him, just as they once were drawn to Satan, trusting the Lie and loving the Lie, before the True God *regenerated* them of *His free will.* "*Which were born* (1) not of blood, (2) nor of the will of the flesh, (3) nor of the will of man, *but of God*" (John 1:13). Whose "will" determines conception and birth, the Father or the born one?

Four

"Irresistible Grace"   **THE CALVINIST VIEW**

Since it is the will of God that those whom He gave to His dear Son in eternity past should be saved, He will surely act in sovereign grace in such a way that the elect will find Christ irresistible. God does not *force* the elect to trust in His Son but rather gives them life. The *dead* human spirit finds the dead spirit of Satan irresistible, and all *living* human spirits find the God of the living irresistible. Regeneration (the work of God) must precede true repentance and faith.

GOD'S WILL IS IRRESISTIBLE

Daniel 4:35—"[Jehovah] doeth according to his will in the army of heaven, and among the inhabitants of the earth: and none can stay his hand, or say unto him, What doest thou?"
Isaiah 46:9, 10—"I am God, and there is none like me, declaring the end from the beginning, and from ancient times the things that are not yet done, saying, My counsel shall stand, and I will do all my pleasure."
Isaiah 55:11—"So shall my word be . . . it shall accomplish that which I please."

GOD WILLS SALVATION OF ELECT

John 6:37—"All that the Father giveth me *shall come to me.*"
John 6:29—"This is the *work of God,* that ye believe on him whom he hath sent."

FATHER BEGETS THOSE HE HAS WILLED

James 1:18—"Of *his own will* begat he us . . ."
John 1:13—"Which were born, not of blood, nor of the will of the flesh, nor of *the will of man,* but (who were born) of God."

ACCOMPLISHED BY GIVING LIFE

John 5:21—"The Son quickeneth *whom he will.*"
Ephesians 2:4, 5—"God, who is rich in mercy, for his great love wherewith he loved us, even when we were dead in sins, *hath quickened us together with Christ* (by grace are ye saved)."
Acts 11:18—"Then hath God *also* to the Gentiles *granted repentance* unto life."

EFFECTUALLY APPLIED BY HOLY SPIRIT

Titus 3:5—"Not by works of righteousness which we have done, but according to his mercy *he saved us, by the washing of regeneration, and renewing of the Holy Ghost."*
2 Corinthians 3:18—"But we all, with open face beholding as in a glass the glory of the Lord, are changed into the same image from glory to glory, even as *by the Spirit of the Lord.*"

***Acts 9—Paul, first known as Saul, is the perfect example of "irresistible grace" and the will of God being achieved for his salvation at the very moment when Saul was leading in the slaughter of the elect, and in strong-willed rebellion against God and His Christ.

Point

THE ARMINIAN VIEW   "Falling from Grace"

The logical conclusion of Arminianism is that since salvation is the result of man's self-determination as he exercises his free will in choosing Christ, man is also responsible to keep himself saved by continuing faith and obedience. Should he after having once accepted Christ decide against Him and eternal life, or should he find the responsibility of living a holy life too great a burden and turn away, he will surely "fall from grace" and be lost.

Galatians 5:4—"Ye are fallen from grace."
Hebrews 6:4–6—"It is impossible for those who were once enlightened, and have tasted of the heavenly gift, and were made partakers of the Holy Ghost, and have tasted the good word of God, and the powers of the world to come, *if they shall fall away*, to renew them again unto repentance, seeing they crucify to themselves the Son of God afresh, and put him to an open shame."
Hebrews 10:26–27—"For if we sin willfully after that we have received the knowledge of the truth, there remaineth no more sacrifice for sins, but a certain fearful looking for of judgment and fiery indignation, which shall devour the adversaries."

WHY WITNESS? WHY BE HOLY?

The *Arminian* often accuses the *Calvinist* of being so scriptural that he takes away all desire to "witness" and live a "holy life." Why should we witness if election is "unconditional," and why should we seek to live a holy life if it is true that "once saved, always saved" (1 Peter 1:15–16)?

The scriptural answers are direct and simple. *We witness* because He has declared, "Ye shall be my witnesses." "We are ambassadors for Christ, as though God did beseech you by us: we pray you in Christ's stead, be ye reconciled to God" (2 Cor. 5:20). *We witness* to the person and work of Christ because it is by the "foolishness of preaching" that God is pleased to save those who believe. However, it is not by our use of psychology, methods, and proper approach that men are saved, but by the power of God through His Word alone (and not our personal "views"). *We witness* because we are "laborers together with God" (1 Cor. 3:9). We preach at His calling. We preach His Word. We plant and water, but God alone gives the increase.

"Shall we continue in sin, that grace may abound? God forbid!" (Rom. 6:1–2). "We are . . . created in Christ Jesus unto good works, which God hath *before ordained* that we should walk in them" (Eph. 2:10). "Wherefore by their fruits ye shall know them" (Matt. 7:20).

Just as a hog loves to wallow in the mire because it is "his nature" to do so, and a lamb flees the mire for the same reason, the reprobate wallow in sin and the elect flee sin. It is the "nature" of each (2 Peter 1:4).

Five

"Perseverance of Saints"   CALVINIST VIEW

The logical conclusion of Calvinism is that since "salvation is of the LORD" and absolutely no part of it is dependent upon any *condition* found in the elect, but is wholly dependent upon the God who has *willed to save those whom He gave to His dear Son,* salvation can never be lost. The saints of God will surely persevere because He has given them His promise that no creature can take them away from Him (including themselves). We shall persevere because He wills to persevere!

PERSEVERANCE DEPENDS ON GOD

Jude 24—"Now unto *him that is able to keep you from falling,* and to present you faultless before the presence of his glory . . ."
Jude 1—"To them that are . . . *preserved* in Jesus Christ, and *called.*"
Ezekiel 11:19—"I will give them one heart, and I will put a new spirit within you; and I will take the stony heart out . . ."
Ezekiel 36:27—"I will put my spirit within you, and cause you to walk in my statutes . . ."
Deuteronomy 30:6—"And the LORD thy God will circumcise thine heart, and the heart of thy seed, to love the LORD thy God with all thine heart, and with all thy soul, that thou mayest live."

NOT DEPENDENT UPON ELECT

1 Peter 1:5—"Who [elect] are *kept by the power of God.*"
2 Timothy 1:12—"I know whom I have believed, and am persuaded that *he is able to keep* that which I have committed unto him against that day."
2 Timothy 4:18—"*The Lord . . . will preserve me unto* his heavenly kingdom."

GOD WILLS SAINTS TO PERSEVERE

Psalm 37:28—"For the LORD . . . forsaketh not his saints, they are preserved for ever."
1 Thessalonians 5:23–24—". . . be *preserved blameless unto the coming of our Lord Jesus Christ.* Faithful is he that calleth you, who will also do it."
Philippians 1:6—"Being confident of this very thing, that *he that hath begun a good work in you will perform it until the day of Jesus Christ.*"

THEREFORE SALVATION CANNOT BE LOST

John 6:39—"This is the Father's will which hath sent me, that of all which he hath given me I should lose nothing."
John 10:26–29—"Ye believe not, because ye are not of my sheep. . . . My sheep hear my voice, and I know them, and they follow me. And I give unto them *eternal* life; and they shall *never* perish, neither shall any man pluck them out of my hand. My Father, *which gave them me,* is greater than all; and no man is able to pluck them out of my Father's hand."
Romans 8:37–39—"We are more than conquerors through him that loved us. For I am persuaded, that neither death, nor life, nor angels, . . . nor things present, nor things to come, nor height, nor depth, *nor any other creature, shall be able to separate us from the love of God,* which is in Christ Jesus our Lord."

Bibliography

Boettner, Loraine. *The Reformed Doctrine of Predestination.* Philadelphia: Presbyterian and Reformed Publishing Co., 1992.

Calvin, John. *Concerning the Eternal Predestination of God.* Translated by J. K. Reid. Louisville: Westminster John Knox Press, 1997.

Edwards, Jonathan. *Freedom of the Will.* Edited by Paul Ramsey. New Haven: Yale University Press, 1957.

Luther, Martin. *The Bondage of the Will.* Translated by J. I. Packer. Grand Rapids: Revell, 1957.

Palmer, Edwin H. *Five Points of Calvinism: A Study Guide.* Grand Rapids: Baker, 1972.

Pink, Arthur W. *Attributes of God.* Grand Rapids: Baker, 1988.

_____. *Sovereignty of God.* Grand Rapids: Baker, 1984.

Sproul, R. C. *Grace Unknown.* Grand Rapids: Baker, 1997.

_____. *Willing to Believe.* Grand Rapids: Baker, 1997.

Spurgeon, C. H. *Election.* Pasadena: Pilgrim Press, 1978.

Steele, David, and Curtis C. Thomas. *Five Points of Calvinism.* Louisville: Presbyterian and Reformed Publishing Co., 1989.

Vance, Laurence M. *The Other Side of Calvinism.* Pensacola: Vance Publications, 1999.